THAI

COOKING CLASS

Authentic Thai Cuisine

HINKLER BOOKS

Contents

Introduction

I began cooking at an early age and food has been my profession and passion ever since. This passion was re-ignited when I first discovered the unique cuisine of Thailand some 15 years ago.

Thai cooking was a revelation to me. Having been classically trained, the ingredients, techniques and philosophy of Thai cuisine required a completely new approach. I found the sharpness and accuracy of the flavours very seductive and once seduced, I set out to discover the intricacies of this wonderful food.

I have spent the past 15 years absorbing its diversity and complexities, and along the way expanding my knowledge and understanding of Thai cuisine. While travelling throughout Thailand and discovering the origins and contexts of the dishes, I have refined my personal approach to and interpretation of this wonderful cuisine, as well as gained a stronger understanding of what people want and need to know so that they too can better appreciate and enjoy Thai cuisine.

Through the understanding I have gained over the years I have come to appreciate the essential balance of Thai food – balance in flavours, textures and ingredients. This balanced approach has been my quest and the fundamental message that I endeavour to pass on to others through cooking classes.

This book is a collection of favourite and popular Thai recipes. I also hope it provides a guide to the fundamental techniques and how to achieve the balance necessary for you to fully appreciate and enjoy Thai cooking.

Paul Blain

Paul Blain

Paul Blain was classically trained in French and Italian cuisine until, in 1990, he joined the original Darley St. Thai in Sydney, Australia under the guidance of David Thompson.

In 1994, Paul established the highly acclaimed Chilli Jam Cafe in Noosa, Queensland, Australia where he developed his own style of innovative Thai, adapting traditional Thai techniques and ingredients to the wonderful array of produce available in the Sunshine Coast region.

Since selling Chilli Jam in 1998 Paul has worked for London based company Tasting Places teaching twice a year at a residential school on Koh Samui, in the Gulf of Thailand. His popular cooking classes have received great reviews in international publications such as the UK's *Sunday Telegraph, London Times,* and *Harpers* and *Queens.* Paul also works as guest chef and presenter at numerous hotels, masterclasses and cooking schools.

In April 2000, Paul opened The Tamarind at Maleny in the Sunshine Coast hinterland, Queensland, Australia.

Finely appointed private accommodation

A unique retreat for couples, The Tamarind overlooks Gardner's Falls and combines a tranquil rural property surrounded by rainforest with finely appointed accommodation and, of course, Paul's exquisite innovative cuisine and popular cooking classes. The Tamarind has received wide acclaim and featured in *Australian Gourmet Traveller, Vogue Entertaining and Travel, Luxury Travel magazine, Cuisine magazine (NZ)* and exposure on *Good Morning Australia, Getaway* and *The Great Southeast.* In 2002 The Tamarind received the Jaguar/Australian Gourmet Traveller Award of Excellence for Gastronomic Travel.

'The Tamarind' – Maleny Queensland

Paul also consults for Anise, a hip new restaurant in Wellington, New Zealand, which opened in June 2002 to great acclaim and continued success.

Paul still finds time to visit Thailand every year teaching, researching and refining his knowledge of Thai cuisine. His passion and knowledge are both extensive and inspiring.

Hua Hin Wharf auctioning the catch

Fresh curry paste stall

Wok cooking at a market stall

Selling fresh Thai vegetables at the markets

Dried & smoked fish & eel stall

Black Pearl Epicure

& Cooking School

Black Pearl Epicure & Cooking School
36 Baxter Street, Fortitude Valley
Brisbane, Queensland
07 3257 2144
www.blackpearl.com.au
vicki.bright@blackpearl.com.au

Babak Hadi's Black Pearl Epicure is Brisbane's most exclusive gourmet retail outlet and home to the internationally renowned Black Pearl Cooking School. Leading purveyors of fine foods, Black Pearl supplies a complete range of fresh and packaged produce to the best restaurants in town.

Cooking school manager Vicki Bright engages Australia's leading chefs for classes that combine education with social interaction. The school caters for individuals with a passion for food and a desire to learn about the wonderful ingredients available and how to use them.

Paul Blain is a regular guest at Black Pearl Cooking School where his Thai Cooking Classes sell out well in advance. The classes provide a rare opportunity to spend time in the kitchen with such a highly regarded chef and learn the intricacies of Thai cooking from a genuine master.

Paul Blain at Black Pearl Cooking School

Fundamentals, Tips and Techniques

Thai cooking, with its wonderful ingredients, distinctive sharpness and accuracy of flavours, is very much a case of the whole being greater than the sum of its parts.

The key ingredients used are on their own often quite strong and have the capacity to dominate. The challenge therefore, is to achieve a balance of these flavours, specifically the four main palates – hot, salty, sweet and sour – without allowing any one flavour to dominate. This marriage of flavours provides the uniqueness of the cuisine and an ongoing challenge for the Thai cook.

This section provides an overview of some of the fundamental techniques and ingredients that help in achieving the required balance .

Hot, Salty, Sweet and Sour

The four main palates in Thai cuisine are hot, salty, sweet and sour.

Hot: Chillies provide the heat in Thai cooking and although it is a required characteristic, the heat also needs to be balanced with the other palates and not dominate the dish or detract from the overall enjoyment of the food. You can modify the quantity of chilli to a level that is comfortable for your palate.

Salty: Fish sauce is the primary provider of saltiness. Sea salt is also used and fermented yellow bean sauce often contributes saltiness. Dark and light soy sauce also have a salty characteristic.

Sweet: Palm sugar and white sugar are used to provide sweetness to both savoury dishes and desserts. Many salads and curries have a sugar component to balance the saltiness and sourness.

Sour: The key ingredient for sourness is lime juice. Lemon juice has a tendency towards bitterness and does not achieve the required taste on the palate. Don't add lime juice to dishes over heat as the heat can turn the juice bitter rather than sour. Always use fresh lime juice. Tamarind is also a source of sourness on the palate, as are vingars, such as coconut vinegar.

Balance of Flavours

Each dish has a required sequence of tastes on the palate. The careful preparation and use of ingredients builds this sequence. Treat the preparation and use of ingredients with care to best release the individual flavours, without allowing them to dominate the dish.

Following are some hints and suggestions of fundamental techniques that will achieve the balance of flavours.

Crispy Frying

Thais often garnish dishes with crispy fried garlic or crispy fried red shallots. Such garnishes provide a subtle flavour and textural contrast to soups and salads. The technique for these garnishes involves frying in hot oil in a large wok and requires vigilant stirring to ensure they don't burn and go bitter.

Once the sliced garlic or red shallots are placed in the hot oil, they will release their water content until they reach a point where they start to crisp and turn golden brown. At this stage remove from heat quickly, drain and then aerate to allow the pieces to crisp.

You can store crispy fried garlic or red shallots for a couple of days in an air-tight container, however they can lose their crispiness very quickly, particularly in humid environments.

Step 1 – Fry garlic in hot oil in wok

Step 2 – Drain off the oil when golden

Step 3 – Shake to drain thoroughly

Step 4 – Aerate to allow pieces to crisp

Curry Pastes

The distinctive quality of Thai curries is due to the complex interaction of fresh woody ingredients, roasted spices and fresh herbs. The flavour achieved from using a freshly made curry paste cannot compare with a commercially prepared paste, which often contain greater quantities of salt and preservative to prolong their life. Fresh pastes, by nature, do not last more than a few days before ingredients start to break down and ferment.

Pastes are best made using a mortar and pestle. A food processor is not as effective in finely grinding woody ingredients and the heat generated can affect the ingredients.

When making the pastes, chop the fibrous ingredients – lemongrass, galangal, ginger, fresh turmeric – into small pieces for a more effective pounding and breakdown. A smooth paste yields a nice smooth textured curry. Likewise if you don't grind pastes smoothly you will end up with a gritty curry.

Roast and grind spices separately to release the flavours, and then combine with the pounded fibrous and wet ingredients to soak up the moisture and create the paste.

Balancing the meal

In Thailand, rice is the staple component of the diet and central to the meal. The dishes are accompaniments to the rice as opposed to the common belief that rice is an accompaniment to a curry.

Served as a single course, a typical Thai meal consists of several dishes shared from the centre of the table. This is a wonderful way to explore and enjoy a range of tastes and dishes. Within a meal, as within each dish, it is important that there is a balance in tastes – hot, salty, sweet and sour – and a balance of ingredients – meats, poultry, seafood and vegetables.

The banquet demonstrated on the accompanying DVD illustrates such a balanced meal. A coconut soup balances a tamarind-based curry, therefore avoiding too much coconut. There is also a balance of meat, seafood and vegetables. Sweetness on the palate is found in the soup, sweet and sour in the curry, hot and sour in the larp and prawn salad, and saltiness in the stir-fried vegetables.

Soups

Dtom Yam Pla

HOT AND SOUR FISH SOUP

Dtom Gati Fak Tong

COCONUT, PUMPKIN AND MUSHROOM SOUP

14/15

Dtom Gati Gung

PRAWN & COCONUT SOUP

Geng Jeut Gai

BROTH OF CHICKEN AND YELLOW BEAN WITH CHOI SUM

16/17

Dtom Yam Pla

HOT & SOUR FISH SOUP (pictured opposite)

INGREDIENTS

SOUP

- 120 g firm fish (skinned and pin-boned) sliced into bite-sized pieces
- 750 ml cold water
- 1 tsp Dtom Yam paste
- 1 stem lemongrass, sliced into 4-6 cm lengths
- 6 kaffir lime leaves, rubbed
- 2–3 medium oyster mushrooms (torn) or small straw mushrooms (whole)
- 50 ml fish sauce
- 40–50 ml lime juice
- 2 small dried chillies, crumbled or whole
- 2–4 red shallots, quartered
- 4–6 thin slices galangal
- 3 ripe cherry tomatoes, halved
- 1/4 cup coriander leaves, loosely packed, to garnish
- 1/2 tbsp crispy fried garlic, to garnish

PASTE

- 2–3 fresh red bird's eye chillies
- 1/4 tsp sea salt

Method

1 In a saucepan, add cold water, Dtom Yam paste, fish sauce, lemongrass, lime leaves, shallots and galangal. Bring to a slow simmer over medium heat for 3 minutes, allowing flavours to infuse. Add mushrooms, tomatoes, fish and chillies. Simmer until fish is cooked – about 1–2 minutes.

2 Remove from heat and season to taste with lime juice.

3 Ladle into a large serving bowl.

4 Serve garnished with coriander leaves and crispy garlic.

Method – To make Dtom Yam paste

- Using a mortar and pestle, grind chillies and salt to a very smooth paste.

Dtom Gati Fak Tong

COCONUT, PUMPKIN AND MUSHROOM SOUP

INGREDIENTS

- 1 cup butternut pumpkin, diced into 1 cm cubes
- 1 medium Swiss brown mushroom, sliced thinly
- 500 ml coconut milk, medium thickness
- 250 ml vegetable stock
- 1/2 tbsp vegetable oil
- 1/2 tsp roasted white peppercorns
- 2 medium coriander roots
- 2–3 roasted small dried chillies, crumbled or whole
- 40-50 ml lime juice, to taste
- 50 ml light soy sauce
- 4–6 slices ginger, thinly sliced
- 4–6 red shallots roasted in their skins until tender, then popped from their skins
- 1/4 cup coriander leaves, loosely packed, to garnish
- 1/2 tbsp crispy fried garlic, to garnish

Method

1 Using a mortar and pestle, pound peppercorns and coriander roots to a robust paste.

2 In a saucepan, warm vegetable oil on a low-medium heat and fry paste until fragrant. Add pumpkin, stirring in. Add coconut milk and stock, red shallots, ginger, dried chilli and mushroom. Bring to a slow simmer and allow pumpkin to soften. Add light soy sauce and simmer a further 2–3 minutes.

3 Remove from heat and stir in lime juice. Correct seasoning with light soy sauce.

4 Serve in a large soup bowl. Garnish with coriander leaves and crispy fried garlic.

Dtom Gati Gung

PRAWN & COCONUT SOUP (pictured opposite)

INGREDIENTS

- 8–10 small green prawns, shelled
- 750 ml of coconut milk, medium thickness
- 4–6 slices galangal, thinly sliced
- 1 lemongrass stem, sliced into 4–6 cm lengths
- 4–6 kaffir lime leaves, rubbed
- 1 medium coriander root, washed and scraped
- 1 tbsp roasted chilli paste
- 1–2 roasted small dried chillies, crumbled or whole
- 30 ml fish sauce
- 40–50 ml lime juice
- 1/4 cup coriander leaves, loosely packed, to garnish
- 1/2 tbsp crispy fried garlic, to garnish

As presented in the accompanying DVD.
Note: 120 g of salmon has been substituted for prawns in the DVD presentation. Firm white fish, without skin and pin-boned can be used.

Method

1 In a saucepan over a medium heat, add coconut milk, galangal, lemongrass, lime leaves, coriander root, roasted chilli paste, dried chilli and fish sauce. Bring to a very slow simmer and infuse for 3–4 minutes. Add prawns and stir gently. Return to simmer. Check that prawns are cooked.

2 Remove from heat and season with lime juice to taste. Correct seasoning with fish sauce.

3 Ladle into a large serving bowl.

4 Garnish with coriander leaves and crispy fried garlic.

Geng Jeut Gai

BROTH OF CHICKEN AND YELLOW BEAN WITH CHOI SUM

INGREDIENTS

- 1 coriander root
- 5 white peppercorns
- 3 red shallots, peeled
- 750 ml Asian stock (chicken or duck)
- 2 tbsp yellow bean sauce
- 1 tbsp oyster sauce
- 1 tsp palm sugar
- 4 kaffir lime leaves
- 100 g chicken thigh fillet, sliced thinly
- 1 cup choi sum, cut into 5cm lengths
- 20 ml fish sauce
- 1 small dried chilli, crumbled, to garnish
- 1/2 tbsp crispy fried garlic, to garnish

Method

1 Using a mortar and pestle pound coriander root, peppercorns and shallots to a paste.

2 In a saucepan, bring stock to the simmer and add paste, yellow bean sauce, oyster sauce, palm sugar and lime leaves. Return to simmer for 1–2 minutes. Add chicken and simmer until cooked. Add choi sum and simmer for another minute until tender. Season with fish sauce.

3 Ladle into a large serving bowl.

4 Garnish with crumbled dried chilli and crispy fried garlic.

Salads

Yam Puu Nahm Jim

HOT AND SOUR CRAB SALAD (pictured opposite)

As presented in the accompanying DVD.
Note: 4-6 (200 g) king prawns, shelled with tails and deveined, have been substituted for crab in the DVD presentation.

INGREDIENTS

SALAD

- 1 cup cleaned crab meat
- 1/2 cup coriander leaves, loosely packed
- 1/2 cup mint leaves, loosely packed
- 1/2 cup Chinese green shallots finely sliced on a long angle into 3-4 cm lengths
- 1 tbsp garlic chives
- 1 tbsp red shallots, sliced thinly lengthways
- 1 tsp lemongrass, finely sliced
- 1 tsp kaffir lime leaves, finely sliced
- 1/4 tsp ground roasted sticky rice, to garnish

DRESSING

- 1 medium coriander root
- whole medium size bird's eye chilli
- 2 small cloves garlic
- 20 ml lime juice
- 15–20 ml fish sauce

Method – To make dressing

1 Using a mortar and pestle pound coriander root, chilli and garlic to a robust paste. Add lime juice then fish sauce. Adjust to taste and set aside. The sauce should be hot, sour and slightly salty.

Method – To make salad

1 In a bowl, combine salad herbs then add crab meat to side of herbs.

2 Spoon dressing over crab meat and gently combine with herbs.

3 Serve on a plate and garnish with ground roasted sticky rice.

Nahm Dtok Neua

SPICY BEEF SALAD

INGREDIENTS

- 120 g trimmed rump
- 4 cherry tomatoes, halved
- 4 red shallots, finely sliced lengthways
- 1/4 cup coriander leaves, loosely packed
- 1/4 cup Chinese green shallots, finely sliced lengthways
- 1/4 cup mint leaves, loosely packed
- 1/3 cup saw-toothed coriander, finely sliced (optional)
- 1 tsp roasted dried chilli flakes
- 1 tbsp ground roasted rice
- 15–20 ml fresh lime juice
- 20 ml thin soy sauce

Method

1 On the char-grill or in a wok, cook rump to medium-rare. Remove and set aside to rest. Slice beef thinly (2-3 mm) and retain all the juices.

2 In a bowl, combine tomatoes, red shallots, coriander, Chinese green shallots, mint leaves, saw-toothed coriander, roasted chilli flakes and 3/4 of the ground roasted rice. Add meat and juices, lime juice and thin soy sauce. Gently combine ingredients.

3 Serve on a plate garnished with remaining ground roasted rice.

Yam Gung Prik Phao Hua Gati

PRAWN SALAD WITH CHILLI PASTE AND COCONUT (pictured opposite)

INGREDIENTS

SALAD

- 6–8 medium green king prawns
- 2–3 red shallots, sliced thinly lengthwise
- 1/4 cup coriander leaves, loosely packed
- 1/4 cup mint leaves, loosely packed
- 1/4 cup Chinese green shallots, sliced finely lengthways
- 1 tsp kaffir leaf, very finely sliced
- 1/4 cup Thai basil leaves, loosely packed

DRESSING

- 1/2 tbsp roasted chilli paste
- 2 tbsp coconut cream
- 1 tbsp lime juice
- 1/2 tbsp fish sauce
- 1 tsp crispy fried garlic, to garnish
- 1 long red chilli, deseeded and finely sliced, to garnish

Method – To make dressing

1 In a bowl, place roasted chilli paste, lime juice and fish sauce. Mix until chilli paste dissolves. Stir in coconut cream.

Method – To make salad

1 In a separate bowl, add red shallots, coriander, mint, basil, green shallots and lime leaf. Peel prawns leaving the tails on. Plunge into simmering water for 1–2 minutes until cooked. Remove and rest.

2 Cut prawns into bite-sized pieces. Combine prawns with salad mixture and gently combine with dressing.

3 Serve on a plate garnished with crispy fried garlic and chilli julienne.

Yam Pla Som Tam

WOK SEARED FISH AND GREEN PAPAYA SALAD

INGREDIENTS

SALAD

- 150 gm firm fish fillet, skin off and pin-boned, cut into 2 cm fingers
- 1 cup green papaya, white flesh
- 1 stem of Chinese green shallots, sliced finely
- 1/4 cup sprigged coriander leaves
- 1/4 cup garden mint leaves
- 1 roma tomato
- 2 green beans, cut into 3cm lengths
- 1/2 tsp roasted rice, to garnish

DRESSING

- 1 garlic clove
- 2–3 small bird's eye chillies
- 20 ml fresh lime juice
- 15 ml fish sauce
- 4–6 dried shrimp
- 1 tsp palm sugar

Method – To make dressing

1 Using a mortar and pestle, pound garlic, chillies and shrimp to a robust paste. Add lime juice and fish sauce. Correct seasoning by adding palm sugar.

Method – To make salad

1 Peel and remove seeds from the papaya. Grate the white flesh on the large shredder side of grater to produce long strips.

2 Heat a little oil in a wok over medium temperature and sear fish fillet until cooked. Put aside to rest.

3 Using a mortar and pestle, gently bruise beans and tomato.

4 Place beans and tomato in a bowl. Add papaya, coriander, mint and shallots. Gently combine salad with dressing.

5 Place bulk of salad on serving plate. Place fish on salad then top with remaining salad.

6 Serve garnished with roasted ground rice.

Yam Nor Mai Farang

ASPARAGUS SALAD WITH LIME, SOY AND CHILLI DRESSING (pictured opposite)

INGREDIENTS

SALAD

- 3–4 fresh green asparagus stems, trimmed and cleaned, cut on a long angle into 3-4 cm lengths
- 1/4 cup torn mint leaves, loosely packed
- 1/4 cup coriander leaves, loosely packed
- 1/4 cup Chinese green shallots, finely sliced on long angle, into 3-4 cm lengths

DRESSING

- 1 roma tomato
- 1 tsp sea salt
- 2 garlic cloves, unpeeled
- 20 ml thin soy sauce
- 10 ml lime juice
- large pinch dried chilli flakes
- 1 tbsp crispy fried red shallots, to garnish

Method – To make dressing

1 Cut roma tomato lengthways into quarters. Cover the cut side with sea salt. Place on a rack and leave overnight.

2 On the char grill, dry-char garlic cloves and tomatoes (cut side down) taking care not to burn. Garlic should be tender. Remove garlic and peel. Place garlic in a mortar and pestle with the tomatoes. Gently pound garlic and bruise tomatoes. Add thin soy sauce, lime juice and chilli flakes and gently combine.

Method – To make salad

1 In a pan, bring some water to the boil and plunge the asparagus cuts. When water returns to the boil, remove asparagus and strain. Asparagus should be tender and crisp.

2 In a bowl, combine asparagus, mint, coriander and Chinese green shallots. Spoon dressing over salad and gently combine.

3 Serve on a plate garnished with crispy fried red shallots.

Yam Makreua Yao

CHAR GRILLED SPICY EGGPLANT SALAD

INGREDIENTS

SALAD

- 3 small finger eggplants
- 1/3 cup Chinese green shallots, finely sliced on a long angle into 3-4 cm lengths
- 1/3 cup coriander leaves, loosely packed
- 3–4 cherry tomatoes, quartered
- 2 red shallots, finely sliced lengthways
- 1/4 cup mint leaves, loosely packed
- 1/2 tsp dried chilli flakes
- 1/2 cup mung bean sprouts
- 2 tbsp cashews, roasted and lightly bruised
- 1 tsp crispy fried garlic, to garnish

DRESSING

- 1 tsp roasted chilli paste
- 10 ml fish sauce
- 15 ml lime juice

Method – To make dressing

1 In a small bowl, place roasted chilli paste, fish sauce and lime juice. Mix until chilli paste is dissolved and paste is smooth.

Method – To make salad

1 Char-grill eggplant with skin on until soft. Cool slightly. Slice in half lengthways and scoop flesh from skin with a spoon. Strip flesh into thin strands with your fingers.

2 In another bowl, combine Chinese green shallots, coriander, tomatoes, red shallots, mint, chilli flakes, bean shoots, cashews and eggplant strands.

3 Add dressing and gently coat all ingredients.

4 Serve on a large plate. Garnish with crispy fried garlic.

Relishes

Lon Bpuu

CRAB AND COCONUT RELISH

Nahm Prik Ong

PORK & TOMATO CHILLI RELISH

28/29

Larp Gai

SPICY CHICKEN RELISH WITH VEGETABLES

Lon Gai Dtow Jiaw

RELISH OF CHICKEN AND YELLOW BEAN

30/31

Lon Bpuu

CRAB AND COCONUT RELISH (pictured opposite)

INGREDIENTS

- 1 1/2 cups coconut cream
- 1/2 tbsp roasted chilli paste
- 20 ml tamarind water (refer recipe page 48)
- 10 ml fish sauce
- 2–3 small dried chillies, crumbled
- 1 tsp palm sugar
- 1 cup crab meat, finely flaked
- 4–6 red shallots, finely sliced lengthways
- 1/4 cup mint leaves
- 1/4 cup Vietnamese hot mint leaves
- 10-15 ml lime juice, to taste

Method

1 In a saucepan, bring coconut cream to simmer for about 1 minute. Reduce until mixture is quite thick. Add roasted chilli paste, tamarind water, fish sauce, small dried chillies and palm sugar. Continue to simmer until mixture thickens. Add crab meat and gently combine. Add red shallots and allow to soften. Stir in mint and Vietnamese mint.

2 Remove from heat and mix in lime juice.

3 Place in a small bowl.

4 Garnish with raw vegetables such as cabbage, wombok, and cucumber. Serve with a few sprigs of coriander, basil and mint on a side plate.

5 Serve with a selection of raw vegetables – torn cabbage or wombok leaves, sliced cucumber slabs, coriander sprigs and tomato slabs.

Nahm Prik Ong

PORK & TOMATO CHILLI RELISH

INGREDIENTS

- 200 g lean minced pork
- 1 tsp small dried chilli flakes
- 1/2 tbsp galangal, finely chopped
- 3–4 red shallots
- 2 cloves garlic
- 1/2 tsp shrimp paste, roasted
- pinch of sea salt
- 2 coriander roots
- 30 ml fish sauce
- 1 tbsp vegetable oil
- 1/2 cup water or tomato juice
- 2 roma tomatoes, roughly chopped
- 1/2 cup torn Vietnamese mint, loosely packed
- 2 tbsp ground roasted sticky rice (refer recipe page 30)

Method

1 Using a mortar and pestle grind coriander root, galangal and salt to a paste.

2 Add garlic, shallots and shrimp paste. Pound to a robust paste.

3 Heat oil in a wok. Add paste and fry until fragrant. Add pork and fry over medium heat separating the grains with the back of a spoon. Continue to fry until liquid from the meat has evaporated. Add chilli and tomato and continue cooking over a low heat, stirring until the tomatoes break down and form a sauce. Add water or tomato juice, a little at a time, as needed. Continue simmering, stirring until sauce becomes slightly thick.

4 Remove from heat and fold through Vietnamese mint and 1/2 the ground roasted rice.

5 Place in a serving bowl and sprinkle with remaining ground roasted sticky rice. Serve with raw vegetables such as cabbage, snake beans, cucumber, wing beans and tomato, cut or torn into spooning-sized pieces.

Larp Gai

SPICY CHICKEN RELISH WITH VEGETABLES

(pictured opposite)

As presented in the accompanying DVD.

INGREDIENTS

- 1 tbsp vegetable oil
- 200 g minced chicken thigh meat
- 1 stem lemongrass, finely sliced into ringlets
- 4–6 red shallots, finely sliced lengthways
- 3 small dried chillies, crumbled
- 1 tbsp fish sauce
- 1/4 cup mint leaves, torn
- 1/4 cup Vietnamese hot mint, torn
- 2–3 tbsp lime juice, to taste
- 3 tsp ground roasted sticky rice (refer method for roasting)
- 3–4 sugar loaf cabbage or wombok leaves
- 1 small continental cucumber
- 4 coriander sprigs
- 1 medium roma tomato

Method – To prepare roasted sticky rice

1. In a dry pan, heat rice over a low flame or roast in an oven until it turns a pale amber. Using a mortar and pestle pound rice to a coarse powder.

Method – To prepare relish

1. In a wok, heat vegetable oil over medium heat. Add chicken mince, stirring to separate, and fry until chicken is lightly coloured.
2. Add lemongrass, sliced shallots and chilli. Season with fish sauce. When shallots have wilted, fold in mint leaves and remove from heat. Add lime juice, and stir in roasted ground rice.
3. Serve with a selection of raw vegetables such as torn cabbage or wombok leaves, sliced cucumber slabs, coriander sprigs and tomato wedges.

Lon Gai Dtow Jiaw

RELISH OF CHICKEN AND YELLOW BEAN

INGREDIENTS

- 150 g chicken mince
- 1 tbsp yellow bean
- 2 garlic cloves
- 2 red shallots
- 1 tbsp vegetable oil
- 1 pinch dried chilli flakes
- 1/3 cup coriander leaves, loosely packed
- 1/3 cup mint leaves, lightly torn
- 1/2 cup coconut cream
- 2 tbsp chicken stock or water

Method

1. Using a mortar and pestle, pound garlic and red shallots to a paste.
2. In a wok, over medium heat, add vegetable oil and paste. Fry until fragrant and a light golden colour. Add yellow bean and stir into the paste. Add chicken mince and work to separate the grains until cooked. Add chilli flakes, coconut cream and stock. Reduce until quite thick. Stir in coriander and mint leaves.
3. Serve in a small bowl on a plate surrounded by a selection of spooning vegetables such as torn cabbage or wombok leaves, sliced cucumber and tomato slabs, and sprigs of coriander and mint.

Curries

Geng Dteng Bpet
RED CURRY OF DUCK WITH PINEAPPLE

Geng Dteng
RED CURRY PASTE

34/35

Geng Gwio Warn Gai
GREEN CURRY OF CHICKEN

Geng Gwio Warn
GREEN CURRY PASTE

36/37

Geng Leuang Pla
YELLOW CURRY OF FISH

Geng Leuang
YELLOW CURRY PASTE

38/39

Geng Mussaman Caa
MUSSAMAN CURRY OF LAMB

Geng Mussaman
MUSSAMAN CURRY PASTE

40/41

Geng Dteng Phad Moo Tua Fak Yaew
DRY STIR FRY OF CRISPY PORK WITH RED CURRY PASTE AND GREEN BEANS

42/43

Geng Bpa Look Chin Gai
JUNGLE CURRY OF GROUND CHICKEN DUMPLINGS AND VINE VEGETABLES

Geng Bpa
JUNGLE CURRY PASTE

44/45

Geng Panang Neua
PANANG CURRY OF BEEF

Geng Panang
PANANG CURRY PASTE

46/47

Geng Hang Lae
NORTHERN STYLE PORK CURRY

Geng Hang Lae
NORTHERN STYLE CURRY PASTE

48/49

Geng Dteng Bpet

RED CURRY OF DUCK WITH PINEAPPLE

(pictured opposite)

INGREDIENTS

- ½ a roasted Chinese duck, boned and thinly sliced (available from Asian supermarket)
- ⅓ cup water
- 350-400 ml coconut cream
- 1 tbsp red curry paste
- ½ tbsp fish sauce
- ½ tbsp palm sugar
- ½ tbsp roasted chilli paste
- 6–8 kaffir lime leaves
- 2 long red chillies, sliced thinly
- 1 tbsp vegetable oil
- 1 cup mushed fresh sweet ripe pineapple
- 1 cup Thai basil leaves, loosely packed

Method

1 In a saucepan or heavy based wok, heat vegetable oil over a low heat and fry curry paste until fragrant. Add palm sugar and roasted chilli paste. Allow to slightly caramelise to enhance the depth of colour. Season with fish sauce. Add chillies and lime leaves, giving leaves a light rub in the hands to release the oil. Stir into paste and soften. Add coconut cream and simmer to bring out the colour and slightly thicken without separating. If the mixture separates add a little cold water and combine. Add duck meat and pineapple and warm through.

2 Remove from heat and fold in Thai basil leaves.

3 Serve in a bowl garnished with a little run of coconut cream or shredded fresh coconut.

Geng Dteng

RED CURRY PASTE

INGREDIENTS (may yield more than needed)

- 5–6 small bird's eye chillies
- 2–3 red shallots
- 3–4 garlic cloves
- ½ tbsp galangal, finely chopped
- ½ tbsp grachai, finely chopped
- 1 tbsp lemongrass, finely shaved
- 1 tbsp Kaffir lime zest, finely chopped
- ½ tbsp coriander root, washed, scraped and chopped
- 7 white peppercorns, roasted
- ½ tsp shrimp paste
- 1 tsp coriander seeds, roasted
- 1 tsp cumin seeds, roasted
- ½ tsp sea salt
- ½ – 1 tbsp sweet paprika powder (optional)

Method

1 In a wok, over low heat, individually roast dry spices to release the fragrance. Using a mortar and pestle, grind each spice separately to a powder. Set aside.

2 Using a mortar and pestle, pound the remaining ingredients to a smooth paste. Add spices and shrimp paste and mix well. To obtain a richer depth of colour, add ½ – 1 tbsp of sweet paprika powder.

INGREDIENTS

- 300 g chicken thigh fillet, cut into bite size pieces
- 2 tbsp vegetable oil
- 2½ tbsp green curry paste
- 2 green chillies, sliced lengthways on an angle into 3-4 cm pieces
- 4–6 medium sized kaffir lime leaves, rubbed
- 1 stem lemongrass, sliced lengthways on an angle into 4–6 cm lengths
- 4–6 green beans or 1 snake bean, cut into 4 cm lengths (available from Asian supermarkets)
- ¼ cup Thai pea eggplant
- ½ cup Thai basil leaves
- 25 ml fish sauce
- 2 cups coconut milk
- ½ cup water (more if necessary)
- ½ tbsp coconut cream

Geng Gwio Warn Gai

GREEN CURRY OF CHICKEN (pictured opposite)

Method

1. In a saucepan, over low heat, fry oil and curry paste for 4–6 minutes until fragrant. Season with fish sauce. Add chillies, lime leaves, lemongrass, beans and eggplants. Fold into paste. Add water and bring to a slow simmer for 3–4 minutes to enhance the colour. Add coconut milk and return to a slow simmer.
2. Place chicken pieces into curry and cook for approx. 4 minutes until curry regains its colour.
3. Remove from heat and stir in Thai basil. Serve in a bowl.
4. Spoon into a large serving bowl.
5. Garnish with a few strands of finely sliced green chilli and kaffir lime leaf and a run of coconut cream over the top.

INGREDIENTS

- 3 tbsp green bird's eye chillies, chopped
- 3 tbsp red shallots, finely chopped
- 2 tbsp garlic cloves, chopped
- 1 tbsp galangal, finely chopped
- 2 tbsp lemongrass, finely chopped into ringlets
- 1 tbsp kaffir lime zest, finely chopped
- 2 tbsp coriander root, washed, scraped and chopped
- 1 tbsp grachai, finely chopped
- ½ tbsp coriander seeds, dry roasted
- ¼ tbsp cumin seeds, dry roasted
- 2–3 cloves
- 10 white peppercorns
- ½ tsp nutmeg, shaved
- ½ tsp turmeric
- 1 tsp shrimp paste, roasted (optional)
- 1 tsp sea salt

Geng Gwio Warn

GREEN CURRY PASTE

Method

1. Using a mortar and pestle, pound lemongrass, galangal, lime zest, coriander root, grachai and sea salt. When ingredients are becoming smooth, add garlic, red shallots, and shrimp paste. Continue pounding to create a smooth paste.
2. Individually dry roast white peppercorns, coriander seeds, cumin seeds and cloves. Grind spices separately to form powders.
3. Slowly add spice powders to paste one at a time, leaving the turmeric until last, adding a little at a time, so as not to take the colour out of the paste. Season with sea salt and continue to pound until all ingredients are smooth and well incorporated.

Geng Leuang Pla

YELLOW CURRY OF FISH (pictured opposite)

INGREDIENTS

- 250 g firm fish fillet, skin off and pin-boned, sliced into 2 cm pieces
- 1 tbsp yellow curry paste
- 4–6 kaffir lime leaves, rubbed
- 1 whole red chilli, sliced lengthways on 20 degree angle
- 3–4 red shallots, halved
- 30 g fresh bamboo, sliced into 1 mm slivers, 4–5 cm long
- 1/2 tbsp fish sauce
- 1/2 cup water
- 250 ml coconut cream
- 1/2 cup Thai basil leaves, loosely packed
- 6 cherry tomatoes, halved
- 30 ml vegetable oil

Method

1 Warm vegetable oil in a pan over low-med heat. Add curry paste stirring with the back of a spoon and fry for 1–2 minutes until fragrant. Stir in lime leaves. Add fish sauce and continue to fry out fish fumes. Stir in chillies and then add cold water. Bring to a slow simmer. Add red shallots and simmer for a further 2 minutes. Add coconut cream and bamboo. Stir and simmer slowly for a further 2 minutes.

2 Place fish in sauce and slow simmer. Turn fish after 2 minutes. If sauce reduces too much add 30 ml of extra cold water at a time, as required.

3 Add cherry tomatoes and simmer for 1–2 minutes longer to finish cooking fish. Remove from heat and fold in torn basil leaves.

4 Serve in a large bowl.

Geng Leuang

YELLOW CURRY PASTE

INGREDIENTS (May yield more than needed)

- 3 tbsp garlic cloves, chopped
- 2 tbsp red shallots, chopped
- 1 tbsp ginger, chopped
- 1 tbsp lemongrass, finely chopped
- 1 pinch sea salt
- 1/2 tbsp coriander seeds, ground
- 1 tsp cumin seeds, ground
- 1/2 tbsp turmeric powder
- 1 tbsp roasted chilli powder
- 1 tsp shrimp paste

Method

1 Using a mortar and pestle, pound garlic, shallots, ginger, lemongrass and salt to a paste. Add coriander, cumin seeds, turmeric, chilli and shrimp paste and continue to pound until all ingredients are smooth and well incorporated.

Geng Mussaman Caa

MUSSAMAN CURRY OF LAMB (pictured opposite)

INGREDIENTS

- 1 kg lamb rump or leg, cut into 2½ cm cubes
- 3 tbsp sweet soy sauce
- 4–5 tbsp Mussaman curry paste
- 3 tbsp palm sugar
- ½ cup tamarind water (refer recipe page 48)
- 4–6 small brown onions
- 1 small sweet potato, cut into 2½ cm cubes
- 1½ litres coconut milk
- 4 cardamom pods, roasted
- 2 Indian bay leaves
- 5 tbsp vegetable oil
- 1 tbsp fish sauce
- 1 cup coconut cream
- 1 tbsp crispy fried red shallots, to garnish
- 2 tbsp peanuts, roasted and ground, to garnish

Method

1 In a bowl, marinate lamb with sweet soy sauce for 10–15 minutes.

2 In a wok, heat 1 tbsp vegetable oil and brown off sweet potato and onions. Remove from wok and set aside.

3 In the same wok, seal and brown the lamb.

4 In a saucepan, place ½ litre of coconut milk, cardamom pods and bay leaves, sweet potatoes and onions and simmer until tender.

5 In another saucepan, heat remaining oil and add coconut cream. Bring to boil, stirring continuously until the cream separates. Reduce heat and add curry paste. Continue to stir until fragrant, making sure it doesn't stick to the pan. Add palm sugar and fish sauce. Fry until paste has a good dark colour. Add tamarind water and simmer for a further few minutes. Add lamb and stir through. Cover lamb with remaining coconut milk. Bring to a slow simmer and cook until lamb is tender, adding more coconut milk if needed. Add sweet potato and onions and warm through.

6 Serve in a bowl.

7 Garnish with ground peanuts and crispy fried red shallots.

Geng Mussaman

MUSSAMAN CURRY PASTE

INGREDIENTS (May yield more than needed)

- 4–6 large dried red chillies, deseeded and roasted
- 6–8 red shallots, unpeeled
- 6–8 cloves garlic, unpeeled
- 1 tbsp galangal, chopped
- 1 stick lemongrass, finely shaved
- ½ tbsp coriander root, chopped
- 1 tsp kaffir lime zest, finely chopped
- ½ tsp white peppercorns, roasted
- 2 tsp coriander seeds, roasted
- 1 tsp cumin seeds, roasted
- ¼ nutmeg, finely shaved
- 2–3 cloves, roasted
- 2 Thai cardamom pods, roasted
- ½ tsp salt
- 2 cm length cassia bark, roasted

Method

1 In a dry wok, over a low heat, add red shallots and garlic and char the skins. Remove and peel. This enhances the colour and contributes a nice smoky flavour.

2 Dry roast separately the peppercorns, coriander seeds, cumin, cloves, cassia bark and cardamom. Grind spices to a fine powder.

3 Using a mortar and pestle, pound salt, chilli, shallots, garlic, galangal, lemongrass, coriander and lime zest to a paste. Add ground spices and continue to pound until all ingredients are smooth and well incorporated.

INGREDIENTS

- 750 g pork belly, skin off and bone out
- 1/2 cup coconut vinegar
- 2 tbsp sea salt
- 50 ml vegetable oil
- 2 tbsp red curry paste (see page 34)
- 1/2 tbsp roasted chilli paste
- 1/2 tbsp palm sugar
- 10 ml fish sauce
- 4–6 kaffir lime leaves, rubbed
- 1–2 long red chillies, cut lengthways on a long angle into 3-4 cm strips
- 1/4 cup chicken stock or water
- 4–6 green beans, cut on a long angle into 3–4 cm pieces
- 1/2 cup Thai basil, loosely packed
- 40 ml thick coconut cream, to garnish
- 1–2 kaffir lime leaves, very finely sliced to garnish
- 1/2 long red chilli, deseeded and julienne, to garnish
- 1 sprig Thai basil, to garnish

Geng Dtaeng Phad Moo Tua Fak Yaew

DRY STIR FRY OF CRISPY PORK WITH RED CURRY PASTE AND GREEN BEANS (pictured opposite)

Method

1 Slice pork across belly into 2 1/2 cm strips. Place in bowl with sea salt and coconut vinegar. Marinate for 20 minutes.

2 Bring steamer to boil and lay marinated pork strips straight, steaming for 15 minutes. Place steamed pork on cooking rack 1 cm apart with roasting tray underneath. Cook in oven (220 degrees c) until pork becomes slightly crisp.

3 Remove and cool for 20 minutes. When cooled, cut into 3 mm thick slices.

4 In a wok, over medium heat, heat vegetable oil. Add sliced pork and fry for 3-5 minutes to render fat and crispen the pork. Add curry paste and stir in with the back of a spoon. Fry for 2–3 minutes until fragrant. Add roasted chilli paste and palm sugar, stirring until palm sugar dissolves. Add kaffir lime leaves and stir. Add fish sauce and fry until fish fumes subside. Add chillies and half the stock or water. Add beans and remaining stock or water, stirring to coat ingredients with curry paste.

5 Remove from heat and fold in torn Thai basil leaves.

6 Serve in a bowl.

7 Garnish with a spoon of thick coconut cream, very finely sliced lime leaf, finely sliced chilli and a sprig of Thai basil.

Geng Bpa Look Chin Gai

JUNGLE CURRY OF GROUND CHICKEN DUMPLINGS AND VINE VEGETABLES

(pictured opposite)

INGREDIENTS

CURRY

- 2 tbsp vegetable oil
- 2 tbsp jungle curry paste
- 500 ml chicken or duck stock
- 30 ml Mekong whisky or bourbon
- 2 tbsp fish sauce
- 2 Thai eggplants, quartered or 8-10 pea eggplants
- 1–2 snake beans, cut into 2 cm lengths
- 30 g bamboo shoots, finely sliced
- 1/2 cup holy basil leaves, loosely packed
- 3 grachai roots, julienne
- 1 cluster of green peppercorns
- 3–5 kaffir lime leaves
- 50 g choko, peeled and finely sliced
- 1 long green chilli, chopped on a long angle into 2 cm pieces

CHICKEN DUMPLINGS

Makes 14–16 dumplings.
Allow 4–5 dumplings per person.

- 200 g chicken mince
- 5 tbsp tapioca flour
- 2 coriander roots
- 1/2 tsp white peppercorns
- 2 garlic cloves
- 1 dsp fish sauce
- 1 egg

Method – to make dumplings

1. Using a mortar and pestle, pound peppercorns, coriander root and garlic to a smooth paste.
2. In a mixing bowl, use a fork to combine chicken mince and paste. Add tapioca flour and continue to combine, adding fish sauce and egg. Mix until well combined. Roll or spoon into quail egg-sized balls.

Method – to make jungle curry

1. In a saucepan, over medium heat, add oil then curry paste and stir fry until fragrant. Add fish sauce and continue stirring for 10-20 seconds. Add whisky, then stock. Bring to a slow simmer and add lime leaves, Thai eggplant, choko, grachai, green peppercorns, beans, bamboo and chilli. Stir all ingredients to cover with stock.
2. Add chicken dumplings making sure they are submerged in the curry. Continue to simmer 3–4 minutes until dumplings are cooked and the flavours developed. Add more stock if needed.
3. Stir in holy basil leaves and serve in a bowl.

Geng Bpa

JUNGLE CURRY PASTE

INGREDIENTS (may yield more than needed)

- 10-15 bird's eye chillies, preferably green
- large pinch salt
- 3 tbsp lemongrass, chopped
- 1 tbsp galangal, chopped
- 3 tbsp red shallots, chopped
- 2 tbsp garlic, chopped
- 1 tbsp grachai, chopped
- 1 tsp roasted shrimp paste
- 1 tbsp coriander root, washed, scraped and chopped

Method

1. Using a mortar and pestle, grind chillies and salt. Then add each ingredient, one at a time, and grind together, adding the harder and drier ingredients first, through to the soft and wet ingredients.
2. Pound to a smooth paste.

Geng Panang Neua

PANANG CURRY OF BEEF (pictured opposite)

INGREDIENTS

- 200 g of trimmed lean rump
- 2 tbsp vegetable oil
- 1½ tbsp Panang curry paste
- 2 tsp roasted chilli paste
- 6 medium kaffir lime leaves
- 1 long red chilli, sliced thinly into 3-4 cm lengths
- 4 medium red shallots, halved
- 1 tsp palm sugar
- 3 tsp fish sauce
- ½ cup water
- 250 ml coconut cream
- ½ cup Thai basil, loosely packed
- 1 tbsp roasted unsalted peanuts, to garnish
- ½ tbsp coconut cream, to garnish
- 1 tsp kaffir lime leaves, finely sliced, to garnish

Method

1 In a wok or on a hot char grill, sear beef for 2½ minutes until medium-rare. Set aside to rest.

2 In a frying pan, warm vegetable oil over a low-moderate heat. Add the Panaeng paste and stir with the back of a spoon to separate. Fry for 1–1½ minutes until fragrant. Add roasted chilli paste and incorporate with Panaeng paste. Add palm sugar, stirring to dissolve. Add lime leaves and chilli, stirring into paste. Add fish sauce and stir to cook out the fumes. Add water and simmer slowly for 1–2 minutes to enhance the colour. Add coconut cream and slowly simmer for 3½ – 4½ minutes to bring back the depth of colour, ensuring not to boil or reduce too much. Reduce heat to low.

3 Thinly slice the beef across the grain into 2–3 mm thick pieces, retaining the juices. Stir beef and juices into simmering curry sauce to coat the meat. Stir in Thai basil leaves and serve in a large bowl.

4 Garnish with roasted peanuts and very finely sliced strips of lime kaffir leaf. Spoon coconut cream over the top.

Geng Panang

PANANG CURRY PASTE

INGREDIENTS (may yield more than needed)

- 6 garlic cloves, chopped
- 3–4 red shallots, chopped
- 1 tbsp lemongrass, finely sliced into ringlets
- 1 tbsp galangal, finely chopped
- 1 tsp kaffir lime zest peel, finely chopped
- 1 tbsp coriander roots, washed, scraped and chopped
- ½ tsp shrimp paste
- ¼ tsp whole white peppercorns
- 1 tsp whole coriander seeds
- ½ tsp whole cumin seeds
- 1–2 whole cloves
- ¼ whole nutmeg, finely shaved
- ¼ star anise, roasted
- 1 cm piece cassia bark, roasted
- 2 tsp roasted red chilli powder
- 1–2 tsp sweet red paprika
- 1 pinch sea salt flakes

Method

1 Using a mortar and pestle, blend galangal, lemongrass, lime zest and coriander roots. As mixture becomes smooth, add garlic, red shallots and shrimp paste, continuing to pound to a smooth paste.

2 Dry roast separately the white peppercorns, coriander seeds, cumin seeds, cloves, star anise and cassia bark. Grind all the spices separately to a fine powder.

3 Add spice powders and nutmeg to paste, leaving chilli powder and sweet red paprika until last. Add chilli powder to taste and finally the sweet red paprika to obtain a greater depth of colour – without increasing the heat.

4 Season with sea salt and continue to pound until all ingredients are smooth and well incorporated.

Geng Hang Lae

NORTHERN STYLE PORK CURRY (pictured opposite)

This dish is part of the Thai banquet in the DVD.

INGREDIENTS

- 1.2 kg pork belly or leg, diced into 2 cm cubes
- 1/2 cup sweet soy sauce
- 1/2 cup vegetable oil
- 6 tbsp curry paste
- 2 tbsp palm sugar
- 3 tsp fish sauce
- 1 litre thick tamarind water (refer recipe)
- 4 heads pickled garlic, peeled and juice retained
- 10–12 red shallot cloves, halved
- 1 knob young ginger, julienne
- 2 tbsp roasted peanuts, to garnish
- 3-4 whole small dried chillies, roasted, to garnish

Method

1. In a bowl, coat pork in sweet soy sauce and marinate for 15–20 minutes.
2. In a medium saucepan, heat oil, add curry paste and fry until fragrant. Add palm sugar and allow to caramelise. Season with fish sauce. Add pork and fry for a further 2–3 minutes, stirring continually to coat the meat. Add 3/4 of the tamarind water and pickled garlic and juice to just cover the pork. Simmer for 1–1 1/2 hours, until pork is tender. Add red shallots and cook a further 5–10 minutes until tender.
3. Just before serving, add ginger julienne. Note: add remaining tamarind water as needed to cover meat during cooking.
4. This curry is quite thick and rich.
5. Serve in a bowl and garnish with crushed roasted peanuts and small roasted chillies. Serve with raw cabbage or wombok, cucumber and thin ginger slices as a side dish (optional).

Method - To make Tamarind Water

1. Soak 150 g of block tamarind in 1 litre of warm water for 4–5 minutes.
2. Work tamarind between your fingers to separate pulp.
3. Strain into container. Discard seeds and fibre.
4. Retain the tamarind water.

Geng Hang Lae

NORTHERN STYLE CURRY PASTE

INGREDIENTS

- 1/4 cup ginger, peeled and chopped
- 1/2 tsp sea salt (optional)
- 1/2 cup garlic cloves, peeled and chopped
- 1/2 cup red shallots, peeled and chopped
- 1 tbsp coriander seeds, roasted and finely ground
- 1/2 tbsp cumin seed, roasted and finely ground
- 1 star anise, roasted and finely ground
- 1 x 2 cm piece cassia bark, roasted and finely ground
- 1–1 1/2 tbsp turmeric powder
- 1–1 1/2 tbsp chilli powder

Method

1. Using a mortar and pestle, pound ginger and salt then add garlic and shallots. Pound to a smooth paste. When paste becomes wet, add coriander, cumin, star anise, cassia and turmeric to bind. Finally, add chilli powder a little at a time to taste.

Steamed and Stir-Fried

Gai Parlow
CHICKEN BRAISED WITH STAR ANISE
52/53

Prik Makreua Mor Din
SPICY EGGPLANT HOTPOT

Hoi Malaeng Puu Mor Din
MUSSEL HOTPOT
54/55

Pat Fak Thawng Gati
STIR-FRIED PAK CHOY WITH PUMPKIN, TURMERIC AND COCONUT

Pat Pak Ruam
STIR-FRIED ASIAN VEGETABLES
56/57

Gai Yang Nam Jim Wan
BARBEQUE CHICKEN WITH SWEET CHILLI SAUCE

Nam Jim Wan
SWEET CHILLI SAUCE
58/59

Pla Nueng Haang Gati
WHOLE STEAMED FISH WITH COCONUT MILK LEMONGRASS AND GINGER

Pat Gai Nam Prik Phao
STIR FRIED CHICKEN WITH ROASTED CHILLI PASTE, CASHEWS AND THAI BASIL
60/61

INGREDIENTS

- 300 g chicken Maryland
- 1 litre duck or chicken stock
- 1 tbsp oyster sauce
- 2 cloves of garlic
- 2 medium coriander roots
- 1/4 tsp whole white peppercorns, roasted
- pinch of sea salt flakes
- 1 tsp Chinese five spice (available in Asian supermarkets)
- 1 x 5 cm stick cassia bark
- 3 star anise
- 1 tbsp sweet soy sauce
- 1 tbsp fish sauce
- 1 tbsp palm sugar
- 1 hard boiled duck or chicken egg, shelled
- 2–3 stems choi sum, cut into 6–8 cm lengths
- 100 ml vegetable oil
- 1 tbsp vegetable oil (for frying paste)
- 1 tbsp coriander leaves, loosely packed, to garnish
- 1/2 tbsp crispy fried garlic, to garnish

Gai Parlow

CHICKEN BRAISED WITH STAR ANISE

(pictured opposite)

Method

1 In a wok, over medium-high heat, heat 100 ml of vegetable oil and sear chicken Maryland. Cook for approx. 5 minutes until skin is crispy. Set aside.

2 Using a mortar and pestle, pound garlic, coriander root, roasted peppercorns and salt to a paste.

3 In a saucepan, over low heat, heat 1 tbsp oil and fry the paste for 2–3 minutes until fragrant and golden. Add oyster sauce, sweet soy sauce, palm sugar, cassia bark, star anise and five spice, stirring to melt the palm sugar. Add chicken, skin side up, and pour enough stock over chicken to cover. Cover with a lid and simmer. After 40 minutes add egg. Continue simmering for 20–35 minutes, adding stock as required, until chicken is cooked. Correct seasoning with fish sauce. Add choi sum and let wilt.

4 Serve in a bowl, placing choi sum as a base with chicken on top. Spoon over the broth, along with the cassia bark and star anise.

5 Cut egg in half and serve to the side of the chicken.

6 Garnish with coriander leaves and crispy fried garlic.

Prik Makreua Mor Din

SPICY EGGPLANT HOTPOT (pictured opposite)

INGREDIENTS

- 350 g or 4 finger eggplants
- 10 ml vegetable oil
- 2 red shallot cloves, sliced finely lengthways
- 5 g ginger, julienne
- 4 large cherry tomatoes, halved
- 1/2 cup vegetable stock
- 10 ml dark soy sauce
- 20 ml thin soy sauce
- 1 large pinch chilli flakes
- 1/2 tsp palm sugar
- 2 oyster mushrooms, torn
- 100 g silken tofu, broken into 3-4 pieces
- 1/4 cup Chinese green shallots, finely sliced lengthways into 3-4cm lengths
- 1/4 cup coriander leaves, loosely packed, to garnish
- 1/2 tbsp crispy fried garlic, to garnish
- 1/2 tsp sesame oil

Method

1. Char-grill eggplant with skin on for approx. 10 minutes or until soft. Cool slightly and slice in half lengthways. Scoop out the flesh with a spoon and tear into strands.
2. In a clay pot, heat vegetable oil and sweat red shallots and ginger. Add eggplant and tomatoes. Add vegetable stock and simmer for 3-4 minutes.
3. In a small bowl, mix superior soy sauce, thin soy sauce, chilli flakes and palm sugar. Mix together until palm sugar dissolves. Add soy mixture to the hotpot stirring to incorporate. Add mushrooms. Cover with lid and cook in oven (220 degrees c) for 10 minutes.
4. Remove from oven and place the silken tofu on top.
5. Garnish with Chinese green shallots, coriander leaves, crispy fried garlic and spoon over the sesame oil.
6. Replace the lid and serve in clay pot.

Hoi Malaeng Puu Mor Din

MUSSEL HOTPOT

INGREDIENTS

- 400 g (15-20) live black mussels
- 2–3 bird's eye chillies
- 3 garlic cloves, peeled
- 2 red shallot cloves, peeled
- 2 coriander roots, washed and scraped
- 1 tbsp vegetable oil
- 3–4 thin slices of galangal, peeled
- 1 stem lemongrass cut lengthways on an angle, into 4–5 cm lengths
- 4–6 kaffir lime leaves
- 2 ripe roma tomatoes, roughly chopped
- 1 cup tomato juice
- 2 tsp fish sauce
- 1/3 cup coriander leaves, loosely packed
- 1/3 cup Chinese green shallots, sliced finely on an angle, into 3–4 cm lengths
- 1/2 tbsp crispy fried garlic, to garnish
- a little water if needed

Method

1. Wash and de-beard the mussels.
2. Using a mortar and pestle, pound chillies, garlic, red shallots and coriander roots to a robust paste.
3. In a clay pot or saucepan, over a medium heat, add the vegetable oil and paste and fry until fragrant and garlic begins to colour. Add mussels, stirring to prevent the paste from burning. Add galangal, lemongrass, lime leaves, tomatoes and tomato juice. Cover with a tight fitting lid and cook for 3-4 minutes. Check that the liquid has not reduced, and if needed, add a little water. Stir. Replace the lid and continue to cook for a few more minutes until the mussels open. Season with fish sauce.
4. Remove any un-opened mussels.
5. Stir in coriander leaves and Chinese green shallots.
6. Pour mussels and sauce into a large clay pot or bowl to serve.
7. Garnish with crispy fried garlic.

Pat Fak Thawng Gati

STIR-FRIED PAK CHOY WITH PUMPKIN, TURMERIC AND COCONUT (pictured opposite)

INGREDIENTS

- 2–3 bulbs pak choy, washed and quartered
- 100 g butternut or blue pumpkin cut into 2 cm x 2 cm x 5 mm pieces
- 2 coriander roots, washed and scraped
- 2 garlic cloves, peeled
- 1 red shallot, peeled
- 4–6 white peppercorns
- 1 tbsp thin soy sauce
- 1/2 tsp turmeric powder
- 1/4 cup coconut cream
- 1 cup vegetable stock
- 1/2 tbsp crispy fried garlic
- 1 tbsp vegetable oil

Method

1. Using a mortar and pestle, pound coriander root, garlic, red shallots and peppercorns to a paste.
2. In a wok, over medium heat, heat vegetable oil. Add paste and stir-fry until golden and fragrant. Add vegetable stock and pumpkin pieces and bring to a simmer. Ensure pumpkin is submerged in the stock. When pumpkin is semi tender, add coconut cream, thin soy sauce and turmeric. Add pak choy pieces and continue to simmer until vegetables are tender.
3. Serve garnished with crispy fried garlic.

Pat Pak Ruam

STIR-FRIED ASIAN VEGETABLES

As presented in the accompanying DVD.

INGREDIENTS

- 3–4 stems choi sum
- 1 bulb pak choy
- 1 bulb bok choy
- 1/2 tbsp vegetable oil
- 3–4 oyster mushrooms, torn
- 1 tbsp yellow bean sauce
- 1/2 cup mung bean shoots
- 8–10 leaves Thai basil, torn
- 1 tsp crispy fried garlic, to garnish
- 1 tbsp water (if needed)

Method

1. Slice Asian greens on a 20 degree angle into 5–6 cm pieces. Wash and drain.
2. In a wok, over high heat, heat vegetable oil, then add oyster mushrooms allowing gill side to colour and crisp. Add yellow bean sauce and fry for a further 5–10 seconds. Add Asian greens, tossing to incorporate mushrooms and sauce. To avoid sticking and burning, add water. This also will help form a small volume of sauce. Cook until tender. Add mung bean shoots and Thai basil, tossing to incorporate.
3. Remove from heat and serve in a bowl. Garnish with crispy fried garlic.

Gai Yang Nam Jim Wan

BARBEQUE CHICKEN WITH SWEET CHILLI SAUCE

(pictured opposite)

INGREDIENTS

- 1 spatchcock (size 8-10), split into quarters
- 1/2 tbsp lemongrass, finely shaved into ringlets
- 1/2 tsp white peppercorns
- 3–4 coriander roots
- 3–4 garlic cloves, peeled
- 1 tsp palm sugar
- 1 tsp fish sauce
- 1 tsp turmeric powder

Method

1 Using a mortar and pestle, grind lemongrass, peppercorns, coriander roots and garlic to a paste. Add palm sugar, fish sauce and turmeric powder, stirring to incorporate.

2 Cut the chicken into 2 thigh pieces and 2 leg pieces. Rub the chicken with paste to cover and leave to marinate in the fridge overnight.

3 To cook chicken, place the pieces on the outside of an oiled char-grill so the chicken heats slowly. This helps the flavour to infuse and the skin to stay intact. Move chicken slowly to the centre of the char-grill to crispen the skin. This should take about 30–40 minutes until cooked.

4 Remove and set aside to rest.

5 Serve arranged on a plate with a side dish of sweet chilli sauce.

Nam Jim Wan

SWEET CHILLI SAUCE

INGREDIENTS

- 6 long red chillies, deseeded and finely chopped
- 2 coriander roots, washed and scraped
- 3–4 garlic cloves, peeled
- 1 tsp salt
- 1 cup coconut vinegar
- 1 cup castor sugar

Method

1 Using a mortar and pestle, pound chilli, coriander root, garlic and salt to a robust paste.

2 In a small pot, add paste, vinegar and sugar. Bring to the boil then reduce heat and simmer for 10–15 minutes until syrup thickens.

3 Set aside to cool before serving.

Pla Neung Haang Gati

WHOLE STEAMED FISH WITH COCONUT MILK LEMONGRASS AND GINGER (pictured opposite)

INGREDIENTS

- 350 g whole fish, scaled and gutted
- 30 cm x 150 cm banana leaf
- 1 tsp roasted chilli paste
- 1 tsp light soy sauce
- 1 cup coconut milk
- 1 stem lemongrass, finely shaved into ringlets
- 50 g ginger, finely sliced into strips
- 1/2 tbsp lime juice
- 1 tsp crispy fried garlic, to garnish
- 3–4 small dry roasted chillies, to garnish
- 1 sprig coriander, to garnish

Method

1. Score the whole fish on an angle at 2 cm intervals on both sides to the bone.
2. In a small bowl, combine roasted chilli paste, light soy sauce and a little coconut milk to dissolve the paste. Add remaining coconut milk and combine.
3. On a plate that fits in the steamer, place a banana leaf and pour a little coconut milk mixture to coat the floor of the plate. Sprinkle about 1/4 of the lemongrass and ginger over the top. Place fish on plate and cover with remaining coconut mix. Sprinkle remaining lemongrass and ginger over the whole fish.
4. Gently place the plate into a boiling steamer and steam for 5-10 minutes. The flesh will separate from the bone when cooked.
5. Pour lime juice over the whole fish, before gently transferring fish on to a serving plate, spooning coconut milk mix back over the top.
6. Garnish with a coriander sprig, crispy fried garlic and dry roasted chillies.

Pat Gai Nam Prik Phao

STIR FRIED CHICKEN WITH ROASTED CHILLI PASTE, CASHEWS AND THAI BASIL

INGREDIENTS

- 250 g of chicken thigh fillet, cut into 4-5 mm thin strips
- 1 tbsp roasted chilli paste
- 4–6 kaffir lime leaves
- 1 long red chilli, sliced on a long angle into 3–4 mm thick lengths
- 1/2 cup whole roasted unsalted cashews
- 1 cup Thai basil leaves, loosely packed
- 1/2 tsp palm sugar (optional)
- 10 ml fish sauce
- 1/3 cup coconut cream
- 1 tbsp vegetable oil
- 3–4 small dried chillies, to garnish

Method

1. In a wok, over a high heat, heat oil and stir-fry chicken until slightly coloured.
2. Add chilli paste, stirring to coat the chicken, and then add rubbed lime leaves and chillies. Stir to combine. Season with palm sugar (optional) and fish sauce and continue to stir-fry for 1–2 minutes until chicken is cooked and chillies are tender.
3. Add coconut cream and return to a simmer. Add cashews and Thai basil, stirring to incorporate.
4. Remove from heat and spoon on to a serving plate.
5. Garnish with small roasted whole dried chillies.

Rice and Noodles

Khao Pat Sapparot

FRIED RICE WITH PINEAPPLE (pictured opposite)

INGREDIENTS

- 1 cup pineapple flesh, finely chopped
- 100 g lean pork, finely sliced
- 200 g green prawns, shelled, de-veined and chopped into small pieces
- 3–4 red shallot cloves, finely sliced
- 2–4 red and green bird's eye chillies, finely chopped
- 1/3 cup Chinese green shallots, sliced finely on a 20 degree angle, lengthways
- 2 tbsp garlic chives, chopped into 1 cm lengths
- 1/2 cup mint leaves
- 2 tbsp roasted unsalted cashew nuts, lightly crushed
- 2 tbsp vegetable oil
- 2 tbsp fish sauce
- 1 tbsp soy sauce
- 2–3 cups cooked jasmine rice, refrigerated overnight
- 1/3 cup mung bean shoots

Method

1. Heat oil in a wok. Add pork and fry until tender and golden. Stir in prawns, red shallots and chillies. Add rice and continue to fry until prawns are cooked and rice is separated and heated through. Add fish sauce and soy sauce. Continue to stir-fry, adding pineapple, cashews, mint, garlic chives, Chinese green shallots and mung bean shoots.
2. Serve on a plate or in half a pineapple cut lengthways with the scooped out flesh used in the fried rice.

Khao Hom Mali

JASMINE RICE

INGREDIENTS

The following is a good average ratio to use for 4 people.

- 2 1/2 cups jasmine rice
- 3 1/2–4 cups water (depending on rice age)

Jasmine rice is a premium grade long grain Thai rice, also known as scented or fragrant rice because of the delicate natural fragrance unique to the rice.

Most Thai cooks vary the water volume according to the age (and dryness) of the rice. New crop rice takes less water to cook, whereas, old crop rice will absorb more water.

Method

1. Rinse the rice at least 3 times in cold running water, waving your fingers through the rice to separate and remove any husks and starch or foreign items. Drain the rice off each time until the water runs clear.
2. Place the strained rice in a medium heavy-based saucepan. Shake the pan so rice is evenly distributed and level. Add the measured water, which should come to a level of 2 1/2 cm (1 inch) above the rice.
3. Cover with a tight fitting lid and quickly bring to the boil, then turn the heat down to very low. Put a layer of foil under the lid if necessary to ensure a tight fit.
4. Cook for 15-20 mins.
5. Check the rice is tender. Rest for 5–7 mins with lid on.
6. Gently wave a fork through the rice in a grid pattern to fluff the rice before serving.

Pat Gung Sen Yai

STIR-FRIED PRAWNS WITH WIDE RICE NOODLES

(pictured opposite)

INGREDIENTS

- 200 g green prawn meat, chopped into bite-sized pieces
- 300 g fresh wide rice noodles (cut into 2½ cm widths)
- 1 tbsp sweet soy sauce
- 1 tbsp light soy sauce
- 1 tbsp yellow bean sauce
- 1 tsp castor sugar
- ½ tbsp oyster sauce
- 2 tbsp vegetable oil
- 3–4 garlic cloves, finely pounded
- 2–3 Chinese kale stems, cut into 2½ cm lengths (available in Asian supermarkets)
- 2–3 Chinese kale leaves, torn
- 1–2 tbsp chicken stock or water
- ¼ tsp ground white pepper
- ⅓ cup mung bean shoots, to garnish
- ⅓ cup coriander leaves, loosely packed, to garnish

Method

1 In a bowl, rub noodles with sweet soy and ½ tbsp of vegetable oil, separating the noodle strands.

2 In a wok, heat ½ tbsp of vegetable oil over a medium heat and stir-fry noodles until the edges brown and they begin to stick. Remove and keep warm.

3 Heat remaining oil in wok. Add pounded garlic and stir-fry until it begins to colour slightly. Add prawns and Chinese kale stems, stirring to incorporate, until prawns are almost cooked. Add noodles and continue to stir. Add light soy sauce, yellow bean sauce, sugar and oyster sauce, stirring to combine. Add Chinese kale leaves and a little stock or water to moisten and prevent sticking, and to wilt the leaves.

4 Garnish with mung bean shoots, coriander leaves and sprinkle with ground white pepper.

Pat Thai

THAI FRIED NOODLES

INGREDIENTS

- 125 g dried thin (2–3 mm) rice noodles
- 3 tbsp tamarind water (refer recipe page 48)
- 2 tbsp fish sauce
- 1 tbsp palm sugar
- 1 tbsp white sugar
- 1 egg
- 1½ tbsp vegetable oil
- 1 garlic clove, finely chopped
- 1 red shallot, finely chopped
- 1 tbsp dried shrimp, pounded
- 1 tbsp preserved turnip, finely chopped
- ¼ tsp dried chilli flakes
- ⅓ cup garlic chives, cut into 2½ cm lengths
- ½ tbsp crushed roasted peanuts
- ½ cup mung bean shoots

TO ACCOMPANY DISH

- 1 wombok leaf, cut into 3–4 pieces
- 3–4 garlic chive stems
- ⅓ cup mung bean shoots
- 1 tbsp crushed roasted peanuts
- 1 tsp dried chilli flakes
- 1–2 lime wedges

Method

1 Soak noodles in hot water for 5–7 minutes or until soft. Drain and set aside.

2 In a bowl, combine tamarind water, fish sauce, palm sugar and white sugar until sugars dissolve.

3 Heat a wok over low heat and add ½ tsp of vegetable oil.

4 Lightly beat egg and pour into wok, rolling to spread egg into a thin crepe, making sure it doesn't colour. Slide egg out of wok and set aside to cool. Roll up and slice thinly to give long ribbon strips. Set aside for garnish.

5 In a wok, over medium heat, add remaining vegetable oil. Fry garlic and red shallots until fragrant and lightly coloured. Add dried shrimp, preserved turnip and mix in. Add noodles and incorporate. Turn up heat and add tamarind mixture. Stir-fry to absorb liquid and slightly colour. Add chilli flakes, garlic chives, peanuts and mung bean shoots, stirring through.

6 Garnish with shredded egg.

7 Serve on a plate with side accompaniments.

Dessert

Khao Niaw Mamuang

WHITE STICKY RICE WITH MANGO

Naam Taan Mamuang

FRESH MANGO CHEEK WITH PALM SUGAR BUTTERSCOTCH

70/71

Khao Niaw Dam

BLACK STICKY RICE

Kanom Mun Gaew

SWEET YAM PUDDING

72/73

Sangkaya Hua Gati

COCONUT CREAM PUDDINGS

Ice-Cream Gati

COCONUT ICE CREAM

74/75

INGREDIENTS (makes 4-6 serves)

- 250 g white sticky rice
- 500 ml coconut cream
- 1 pandanus leaf
- 150 g castor sugar
- 1 tsp salt
- 2–4 star anise
- 1–2 pieces cassia bark

GARNISH

- 3–4 thick slices fresh ripe mango per person
- 1 tbsp coconut cream per serve
- 1/2 tsp roasted sesame seeds per serve

Serve rice in large quenelles, topped with sliced mango, coconut cream and toasted sesame seeds.

Khao Niaw Mamuang

WHITE STICKY RICE WITH MANGO (pictured opposite)

Method

1 Rinse the rice in several changes of water, then cover with 5 cm cold water and half the pandanus leaf and soak overnight. Rinse rice and drain.

2 In the steamer base, half fill with water and add half the star anise and cassia bark.

3 Mould the rice into a hill on the steamer tier and steam for about 20 minutes or until tender.

4 In a stainless saucepan, place coconut cream, salt, sugar and remaining pandanus, star anise and cassia bark. Stir over a low heat until sugar dissolves. Set aside to allow spices to infuse.

5 When rice is cooked turn into a bowl and pour strained coconut cream over the top, cutting through the rice with your spoon to allow the liquid to absorb.

6 Cover the bowl and set aside so rice absorbs the coconut – this should take about 20–25 minutes.

INGREDIENTS (makes 1 serve)

- 1/2 ripe fresh mango
- 1 tsp castor sugar
- 1 tsp cold water
- 1 tbsp palm sugar
- 1 tbsp coconut cream
- 1 tsp unsalted butter
- 1/2 tsp toasted sesame seeds
- 1 lime wedge

Note: Mango can be substituted with custard apples or bananas

Naam Taan Mamuang

FRESH MANGO CHEEK WITH PALM SUGAR BUTTERSCOTCH

Method

1 Cut mango lengthways. With a large kitchen spoon, scoop the flesh (cheek) out of its skin in one piece.

2 Place in the centre of a serving dish and set aside.

3 In a small pan, over low heat, sprinkle castor sugar evenly. Allow to liquefy and turn a light amber colour. At this point, to avoid burning, add cold water. This will lift the caramel from the pan.

4 Add palm sugar and simmer to combine with the caramel. Add coconut cream and simmer until slightly thick. Add butter and swirl in the sauce to melt and give a sheen. Be careful not to split the sauce.

5 Spoon sauce over the mango cheek and sprinkle with toasted sesame seeds. Garnish with a lime wedge and serve.

Khao Niaw Dam

BLACK STICKY RICE (pictured opposite)

INGREDIENTS

- 2 cups black sticky rice
- 1 pandanus leaf, knotted
- $^1/_2$ cup palm sugar
- $^1/_4$ dried mandarin peel (available in Asian supermarkets)
- 2 cups coconut milk
- 1 tsp salt
- 12 mandarin segments
- 1 tbsp toasted sesame seeds
- 2 tbsp thick coconut cream

Serve warm or at room temperature on the day it is made. Serve in small bowls with coconut cream, mandarin segments and toasted sesame seeds.

Method

1 Place rice in a bowl and rinse several times, then cover with 5 cm cold water and soak overnight.

2 Drain rice and rinse again several times, running your fingers through to remove excess starch. Drain.

3 In a saucepan with a lid, add rice, pandanus leaf, mandarin peel and 5 cups cold water. Bring to boil, then reduce and simmer for 30–40 minutes, stirring occasionally to avoid sticking or scorching. The liquid should be almost fully absorbed and form a thick sauce.

4 Check to see rice is tender. Remove pandanus leaf and mandarin peel. Stir in palm sugar, salt and coconut milk, allowing sugar to dissolve. Reduce heat to lowest setting and replace lid. Cook for a further 5-10 minutes.

5 Remove from heat and rest with lid partially off for 5–10 minutes.

Kanom Mun Gaew

SWEET YAM PUDDING

INGREDIENTS (makes 8 serves)

- 800 g raw sweet gold potatoes, peeled and chopped (should produce 3 cups puree)
- 15 g ginger, peeled and cut into shards
- 1 x 6 cm piece cassia bark
- 10 x 62 g eggs
- 2 cups palm sugar (approx. 500 g)
- 1 cup shredded coconut
- 2 cups thick coconut cream rice flour
- 1 tbsp vegetable oil
- 2 tbsp castor sugar
- 1 cup crispy fried red shallots

To serve, cut in 2 inch squares and top with crispy fried red shallots.

Note: Ideal with coconut ice-cream.

Method

1 Pre-heat oven to 220 degrees c. Before cooking pudding, place a 20 x 20 cm non-stick baking tin in the oven to heat for 10 minutes.

2 Peel and cut sweet potato into $2^1/_2$ cm cubes. Steam for 15 minutes until soft. Place sweet potato in a pot and mash. Add cassia bark and ginger shards.

3 Return pot to a low heat and cook mixture for approx.10 minutes until dry. Stir continuously to avoid scorching.

4 Melt palm sugar and add coconut cream and lightly beaten eggs. Mix well and strain. Add potato mix and incorporate.

5 Over a low heat, stir mixture continuously for approx. 10 minutes to thicken to a smooth, firm consistency. Avoid clumping and scorching. Remove from heat. Stir in shredded coconut, rice flour and vegetable oil. Pour mixture into hot, well oiled cake tin (this helps with base crusting), and smooth the top with oiled spatula. Evenly sprinkle with sugar.

6 Place in oven at $^3/_4$ level and bake for 30–40 minutes until golden and slightly pulling away from the sides of the tin. Top should be caramelised.

7 Remove and rest. Serve at room temperature.

Sangkaya Hua Gati

COCONUT CREAM PUDDINGS (pictured opposite)

INGREDIENTS (makes 10 individual puddings)

- 380 ml pouring cream
- 300 ml pouring cream for whipping
- 600 ml thick coconut cream
- 1 cup castor sugar
- 12½ g gelatine leaves
- ¼ fresh coconut
- fresh mango (½ mango per person)

To serve, remove puddings from fridge and place ramekin on a serving plate. Sprinkle the top of puddings with coconut chips and serve.

Method

1 In a saucepan over a low heat, warm 380 ml of cream and sugar until sugar dissolves.

2 In a bowl, soften gelatine leaves in cold water. Do not dissolve. Once soft and pliable, gently squeeze out the excess water and add gelatine to sugar and cream mixture. Gently stir to dissolve over a low heat.

3 Put 600 ml of thick coconut cream into a stainless mixing bowl and strain gelatine mixture into coconut cream. Stir gently. Place mixture in fridge until it starts to 'hang'. Do not set. To test, gently shake the bowl. The mixture should form a wave effect across the bowl.

4 Soft whip 300 ml pouring cream and gently fold into coconut cream mixture. Carefully spoon into 150 ml ramekins and place in fridge to set. Puddings should set in 3–4 hours.

5 Break open coconut and drain liquid. Spoon flesh out of half a coconut and remove any brown sections attached to coconut meat. Place coconut on a bread board and using a stable vegetable peeler, shave downwards to obtain nice long chips of coconut. Place coconut chips on a stainless steel tray in a low oven (120 degrees c) for about 10 minutes until chips are crisp and lightly brown. Do not burn.

Ice-Cream Gati

COCONUT ICE CREAM

INGREDIENTS
(makes 2 litres)

- 1 litre coconut cream
- 600 ml heavy cream
- 10 egg yolks
- 1½ cups castor sugar
- 1 pandanus leaf, knotted
- 1 x 5 cm stick cassia bark
- 2 star anise
- 1 tsp salt

Method

1 In a saucepan, place coconut cream, cream, half the sugar, pandanus leaf, cassia bark, star anise and salt. Slowly heat for approx. 20–30 minutes to infuse ingredients. Do not let simmer. Set aside to cool slightly. Strain.

2 In a double boiler, place remaining sugar and egg yolks. Whisk mixture to the sabayon stage, and slowly pour in the coconut mixture. Continue to stir until slightly thickened. Avoid scorching which turns mixture bitter. Remove and cool, stirring occasionally to avoid skinning.

3 In an ice cream machine churn mixture to appropriate consistency. Remove ice-cream and store in an airtight container in freezer until needed.

DRY	
metric (grams)	imperial (ounces)
30 g	1 oz
60 g	2 oz
90 g	3 oz
100 g	3½ oz
125 g	4 oz
150 g	5 oz
185 g	6 oz
200 g	7 oz
250 g	8 oz
280 g	9 oz
315 g	10 oz
330 g	11 oz
370 g	12 oz
400 g	13 oz
440 g	14 oz
470 g	15 oz
500 g	16 oz (1 lb)
750 g	24 oz (1½ lb)
1000 g (1 kg)	32 oz (2 lb)

LIQUIDS	
metric (millilitres)	imperial (fluid ounces)
30 ml	1 fl oz
60 ml	2 fl oz
90 ml	3 fl oz
100 ml	3½ fl oz
125 ml	4 fl oz
150 ml	5 fl oz
190 ml	6 fl oz
250 ml	8 fl oz
300 ml	10 fl oz
500 ml	16 fl oz
600 ml	20 fl oz (1 pint)
1000 ml (1 litre)	32 fl oz

Conversions

Measurements differ from country to country, so it's important to understand what the differences are. This Measurements Guide gives you simple 'at-a-glance' information for using the recipes in this book, wherever you may be.

Cooking is not an exact science – minor variations in measurements won't make a difference to your cooking.

Equipment

There is a difference in the size of measuring cups used internationally, but the difference is minimal (only 2–3 teaspoons). We use the Australian standard metric measurements in our recipes:

1 teaspoon	5 ml
½ cup	125 ml
4 cups	1 litre
1 tablespoon	20 ml
1 cup	250 ml

Measuring cups come in sets of one cup (250 ml), ½ cup (125 ml), ⅓ cup (80 ml) and ¼ (60 ml). Measuring spoons come in a set of four and should be used for measuring dry and liquid ingredients. When using cup or spoon measures always make them level (unless the recipe indicates otherwise).

Dry versus wet ingredients

While this system of measures is consistent for liquids, it's more difficult to quantify dry ingredients. For instance, one level cup equals 200 g of brown sugar; 210 g of caster sugar; and 110 g of chilli powder, coriander seeds, cumin.

When measuring dry ingredients such as dry spices don't push them down or shake them into the cup. It is best just to spoon them in until the desired amount is reached. When measuring liquids use a clear vessel indicating metric levels.

Always use large eggs (62 g) when eggs are required in a recipe.

1 cup jasmine rice	=	215 g
1 cup coriander seeds	=	85 g
1 cup chilli powder	=	110 g
1 cup palm sugar	=	250 g

(All 1 tablespoon)		
Coriander seeds	=	7 g
Cumin seeds	=	10 g
Chilli powder	=	10 g
White pepper	=	13 g
Cardamom pods	=	12 g
Whole cloves	=	8 g
Turmeric powder	=	11 g

Glossary of ingredients

Paul Blain in his Asian herb garden

Bamboo Shoots – Edible shoots of the bamboo plant. Use fresh shoots where available. Also available in jars and cans from Asian supermarkets.

Basil –

Thai Basil (bai horopha) has a purple tinge to leaves and stems and a distinctive aniseed aroma and flavour.

Holy Basil (bai ka-phrao) is a strong aromatic basil which smells like cloves. Used in stir-fries or deep-fried as a garnish.

Lemon Basil (bai maeng-lak) has a small leaf with distinctive lemon citrus aroma and taste. Used with seafood stir-fries and hotpots.

Bok Choy – Green leafy Asian vegetable. Available from Asian supermarkets or greengrocers.

Cardamom – Dry spice used in Muslim-influenced curries such as Mussaman.

Cashew Nuts – Sweet nut used in stir-fries. Raw nuts are roasted in oil and unsalted.

Cassia Bark – Similar to cinnamon but with more of an earthy quality and larger coarser quills, it is used as a dried spice in some curry pastes and to infuse flavour in some desserts. Available from Asian supermarkets.

Chillies –

Long Chillies, also known as dragon chillies, are not as hot as the small varieties. Both red and green are used.

Bird's Eye Chillies are the commonly used, distinctively hot, small Thai chillies. Both red and green are used.

Dried chillies either long or bird's eye, imparts a smokey quality to the dish. Available whole, in flakes or as a fine powder from Asian supermarkets.

Choi Sum – A green leafy Asian vegetable which can be sourced from Asian supermarkets or greengrocers.

Cloves – Small brown dried bud of the clove tree. A distinctive and strong spice used in some curry pastes in small quantities.

Coconut –

Coconut Cream is the thick rich liquid extracted from soaking coconut flesh in water and then squeezing the flesh in muslin to extract the cream.

Coconut Flesh is the fresh white 'meat' of the coconut. Used grated or shaved in desserts.

Coconut Milk is a diluted version of coconut cream. Available in cans or you can make better quality milk by diluting a good quality coconut cream.

Coriander – Also known as Cilantro, fresh coriander leaves are used in salads, soups, stir-fries and as a garnish. Coriander roots are used in pastes and dressings. The small, round, aromatic Coriander seed is roasted and ground for curry pastes.

Cumin – Cumin seeds are distinctively aromatic and are roasted and ground for curry pastes.

Dried Shrimp – Very small shrimp are dried and preserved and impart a distinctive saltiness and flavour to stir-fries, curry pastes and some salads. Available in packets from Asian supermarkets.

Glossary of ingredients *(continued)*

Eggplant –
Long Eggplant, also known as finger eggplant, is long, thin and either green or purple.

Apple Eggplant are about the size and shape of a golf ball and either white, green or purple.

Thai Pea Eggplant are clusters of pea-like fruits that have a distinctive bitter quality and are often used in green and jungle curries.

Fish Sauce – Made from small salted fish, fish sauce is the main contributor of saltiness to Thai dishes. It is extremely pungent and should be stored in refrigerator after opening. A good amber colour (not dark) indicates freshness.

Galangal – Related to the ginger family, galangal has a distinctive citrus spiciness and is a major ingredient in pastes, soups and dressings.

Garlic –
Thai Garlic is smaller than European garlic, although both are suitable.

Crispy Fried Garlic is used as a garnish in many dishes. Available in packets from Asian supermarkets or refer to page 9.

Pickled Garlic Cloves are used in some curries and salads and available in jars from Asian supermarkets.

Garlic Chives – Long flat leaves which impart a garlic aroma when cut and have a distinctive garlic flavour. Sold in bunches from Asian supermarkets.

Ginger – Aromatic rhizome used in curries, stir-fries and steamed dishes. Ginger becomes woody as it ages so use fresh young ginger.

Grachai – Also known as 'wild ginger' or 'Chinese keys'. Related to ginger and galangal, these smaller rhizomes are used in some curries and impart a distinctive peppery flavour. Available in jars of brine from Asian supermarkets.

Kaffir Lime – A distinctive and aromatic citrus tree, the Thais use the leaves either lightly crushed in soups and curries or very finely sliced in salads. The fruit has a thick wrinkled skin with very little juice, but the zest is used in curry pastes.

Lemongrass – The fibrous stem is used fresh and finely chopped or in larger pieces to infuse flavour. Imparts a fresh citrus flavour.

Limes – The major contributor of sourness to dishes. Tahitian limes are more readily available than Thai limes and are the best substitute. Don't substitute with lemons, which are more bitter than sour.

Mint – Commonly used in salads imparting a fresh clean flavour.

Vietnamese Mint, also known as hot mint – has a distinctive peppery flavour in the leaves. Available fresh from Asian supermarkets.

Mung Bean Sprouts – Used in stir-fries, soups and salads and readily available from most supermarkets or greengrocers.

Mushrooms – A range of varieties are used in soups and stirfries – oyster, Swiss browns and shitake mushrooms are available fresh from greengrocers and Asian supermarkets. Shitake mushrooms are also available dried from Asian supermarkets and can be used after soaking in water.

Noodles – Noodles were introduced to Thailand from China and are often eaten at lunchtime.

Rice Noodles come in a range of widths – wide line (sen yai) rice noodles are produced from large sheets and cut into 2 cm wide ribbons. Small line noodles (sen lek) are 3-5 mm wide. Available both fresh and dried from Asian supermarkets.

Egg Noodles (ba-mii) are available dried or fresh from Asian supermarkets and in a range of widths.

Mung Bean or Vermicelli Noodles (wun sen) are very fine glass like noodles available dried from Asian supermarkets.

Nutmeg/Mace – Used as a dried spice the outer casing is shaved and used in some curry pastes. Whole nutmegs are available from Asian supermarkets.

Oyster Sauce – Used in stir-fried and steamed dishes it is readily available from Asian supermarkets.

Pak Choy – Green leafy Asian vegetable. Available from Asian supermarkets or greengrocers.

Palm Sugar – Palm sugar contributes sweetness to dishes. Palm sugar is sold as a solid mass either in cakes or in jars. Thai palm sugar is much lighter in colour and has a more subtle flavour than the darker versions from Indonesia and Malaysia.

Pandanus Leaves – Long fibrous green leaves from an Asian pandanus plant. Used to wrap food or in desserts to infuse its distinctive slightly nutty flavour. Not always readily available fresh. Frozen leaves and small bottles of essence are suitable substitutes.

Papaya (green) – The un-ripe white flesh of the papaya is used finely sliced or grated in salads soups and curries. Can be sourced through Asian supermarkets and greengrocers.

Paprika Powder – Sweet paprika powder is a very fine, deep red coloured powder used in making some curry pastes. Available in packets from Asian supermarkets.

Peppercorns – White and black peppercorns are used as a dried spice in many curry pastes and stir-fry pastes. Clusters of fresh green peppercorns are used in stirfries. Both can be sourced from Asian supermarkets.

Red Shallots – Also known as Asian shallots. Similar in appearance to garlic, with red skin and bulbs. Substitute with small Spanish red onions if unavailable.

Rice – The staple diet of the Thais, Jasmine rice is widely produced and consumed. White Sticky Rice is eaten steamed with traditional dishes in the North. Both white and black (un-refined) sticky rice is eaten for dessert throughout Thailand.

Roasted Chilli Paste *(in soybean oil)* – An important ingredient in a range of dishes. Available in jars in soybean oil from Asian supermarkets.

Shrimp Paste (Kapi) – This pungent paste is made from salted and fermented shrimp. The paste is often smeared on a banana leaf and dried in the sun or an oven then crumbled. This makes it less pungent.

Soy Sauce – Both dark and light soy sauce contribute saltiness and can replace fish sauce for vegetarians. Sweet soy (ketchup manis) is used to marinate meats and in stir-fried dishes.

Star Anise – Small dried star shaped pods with a distinctive aniseed aroma and flavour. Used as a dried spice in curry pastes and whole in some braised dishes and desserts. Available in packets from Asian supermarkets.

Tamarind – The pulpy fruit from the pod of the Tamarind tree. Contributes a sweet sour flavour to dishes. Available in blocks from Asian supermarkets

Tapioca Flour – A fine flour from the cassava root, used as a thickening agent.

Tofu – Also known as bean curd. Available as silken (soft) and firm forms from Asian supermarkets.

Turmeric – A rhizome similar to ginger and galangal. Used fresh or as a dried powder.

Vinegar – Coconut vinegar is the most common and is a slightly opaque liquid used for marinating meats, dressings and dipping sauces. Rice vinegar and Chinese red vinegar are also used.

Yellowbean Sauce *(soybean paste formula one)* – Produced from fermented yellow soybeans. This thick sauce contributes to the saltiness of dishes. Can be used in soups, relishes and stir-fries.

the TAMARIND
BUNGALOWS • RESTAURANT • COOKERY RETREAT

For further information contact Paul Blain:
enquiries@thetamarind.com.au
www.thetamarind.com.au
Tableware courtesy of BAYSWISS, Pacific Fair, Qld

Coordinator: Karen Moores
Art Director: Karen Moores
Graphic Designer: Susie Allen
Photography: Glenn Weiss
Editor: Stefan Treyvaud

Thai Cooking Class
Published in 2004 by Hinkler Books Pty Ltd
17–23 Redwood Drive
Dingley VIC 3172 Australia
www.hinklerbooks.com

ISBN: 1 7415 7000 X
Printed and bound in China